"Love makes the world go round or at least we wish it did. Greg Popcak knows it does and will persuade you that love can be true…for you. Popcak's pen is trained by thousands of hours of clinical experience, rich study, deep prayer, and the experience of being a husband and a father. He is a man who knows how to love and is loved. He's also a masterful communicator who knows the power of stories. Get out and find *How to Find True Love*. If you don't need to read it, rest assured, 90 percent of the rest of us do. Hand it out to your sister, son, sitter, surgeon, or soprano in the church choir. Dr. Popcak writes with a fresh, universally accessible style that can't fail to enrich all who read. Fear not, love will not only find a way, it will become your way after reading *How to Find True Love*."

Al Kresta, President/CEO Ave Maria Radio and host "Kresta in the Afternoon"

"Greg Popcak has a great gift for expressing the deepest truths of human life in clear, down-to-earth language. In *How to Find True Love* he invites us to move beyond the superficial images so popular in our culture and to look into the heart of a great mystery: that we were created for love, that real love changes even those of us who don't want to be changed by it, and that it is only by having the courage to be open to real love, in all its forms, that we become the people God wants us to be. This is a beautiful and very helpful book."

Dan Connors, Editor-in-Chief, *Catholic Digest*

How to Find True Love

Gregory K. Popcak, Ed.D.

A Crossroad Book
The Crossroad Publishing
Company
New York

The Crossroad Publishing Company
www.CrossroadPublishing.com

In continuation of our 200-year tradition of independent publishing, The Crossroad Publishing Company proudly offers a variety of books with strong, original
voices and diverse perspectives. The viewpoints expressed in our books are not
necessarily those of The Crossroad Publishing Company, any of its imprints or of
its employees. No claims are made or responsibility assumed for any health or
other benefit.

Printed in the United States of America.

The text of this book is set in Berkeley
The display face is Tempus Sans ITC

Project Management by
Crossroad Publishing Company
John Jones
For this edition numerous people have shared their talents and ideas, and we
gratefully acknowledge Gregory K. Popcak, who has been most gracious during
the course of our cooperation. We thank especially:
Project Editor: John Jones Cover design: George Foster
Text design: Michael Winegardner
Web Fusion Text Art Editing: Maggie P. Duffey
Message development, text development, package, and market positioning by
The Crossroad Publishing Company

Library of Congress Cataloging-in-Publication Data
Popcak, Gregory K.
  How to find true love / Gregory K. Popcak
     p. cm.
  ISBN 978-0-8245-2693-1
  1. Love. 2. Friendship. I. Title.
  BF575.L8P67 2012
  646.7'7--dc23   2012022611

Books published by The Crossroad Publishing Company may be purchased at
special quantity discount rates for classes and institutional use. For information,
please e-mail sales@crossroadpublishing.com

Table of Contents

Give Love
Forever After

A Really Big Hit

Not long ago, I attended a wedding reception where the DJ played a game to find out which couples had been married the longest. He called all the married couples onto the dance floor. One by one, as they were dancing, the DJ invited couples "married 'x' years or less" to leave the floor. One year, 5 years, 10 years, 20 years, 30 years. Each time the DJ called out a higher number, more and more couples left the floor until just one couple, Hank and Bonnie, married 54 years, remained.

The DJ asked if they had a song they wanted him to play, and they requested *Unchained Melody*. A few people there wondered why a couple married for over half a century would choose a song from *Ghost*, a movie that came out in 1990. Some of the older couples remembered that the Righteous Brothers' hit record first appeared in 1965.

But the couple explained that the original recording was even earlier than that, from 1955—recorded by Todd Duncan, from the movie *Unchained*. They told the DJ that when Hank asked his wife to marry him at the 1955 county fair, a band was playing the song in the background. At the time, she was 18 and he was 20. Now 74 years old, Hank took the microphone from the DJ and said, "Of course, that song went on to be a really big hit. Just like my marriage to Bonnie."

As the elderly couple took the floor to dance to their song, it was as if the years melted away. They held each other, and you could tell that as she rested her head next to his, she still felt like that girl fresh out of high school, clinging to the boy she loved. The way he held her spoke volumes about all they'd been through together and the years they hoped they would continue to share. And as the DJ invited the newlyweds to join the older pair on the dance floor, the circle was complete.

Sometimes a song seems to articulate the power of our love for each other like nothing else. Music evokes feelings that time cannot touch. Dancing to *Unchained Melody* after 54 years of committed and loving marriage,

Hank and Bonnie shared one of the secrets of finding true love: remembering the first sparks of romance and keeping them alive.

Why are more songs written about *love* than any other theme? What is it about finding true love that inspires so many notes? When it comes to love, it doesn't matter whether you're the reincarnation of Pavarotti or can't even carry a tune. Sometimes, as Jim Croce put it, we just "have to say 'I Love You' in a song."

St. Augustine, an early Christian writer, once observed that to sing is to pray twice. Music intensifies any experience. When we sing love songs, it gives us a chance to tell someone we love them twice. Music also marks memories. For reasons not completely understood, music wires the brain in such a way that when we hear a song, the feelings and experiences associated with that song come rushing back to us so that we can experience them over and over as if for the very first time. Perhaps that's why, like Hank and Bonnie, so many couples have a song that reminds them of the first time they knew they were in love, a song they can return to time after time.

Music also reminds us that true love is never limited to

ordinary words. The stories in this book will show you countless ways you can experience and give true love. Whether it's the romantic love of a couple, family love for your children, parents, and brothers and sisters, or love that you share with friends, coworkers, and even strangers, remember that the fairytales you grew up with are only part of the story. You can find true love in all times, all places, and with all people—as long as your heart remains open.

For Six Months, Forever

"We promised that we would be married for 6 months for the rest of our lives."

Darren and Yvonne were explaining to me the secret of their enviable marriage. Everybody is good at something, and Darren and Yvonne seem to excel at creating a beautiful life together. They have the sort of marriage that seems effortless. They're affectionate with each other without being awkward, complimentary without being cloying, and they celebrate a friendship that never feels forced. Even their kids and their kids' friends notice—in a good way.

"The other day," said Yvonne, "Michaela, our 12-year-old, had some friends over. I was making them a snack when Darren came in and gave me a kiss. Nothing super passionate, just a thoughtful kiss. The girls must have seen us because later Michaela told us that her friend said to her, 'Wow, your mom and dad must really love each other. My parents never do that.' I apologized if we embarrassed her, but she just said, 'No, I like that you guys like each other!'"

What's their secret?

"Years ago, we went on a camping trip," Darren recalled. "This was before the kids were born. Yvonne and I were sitting by the campfire, holding hands and kissing. I remember her just resting her head on my shoulder. Well, a kid from the next campsite came over—we'd met the family earlier that day—and asked us, 'How long have you guys been married?'

"I thought I must have heard her wrong, so I said, 'What?' and the little girl repeated it. 'How long have you guys been married?' I looked at Yvonne and said, 'Three years. Why?' And the little girl declared, 'Mom said that you guys must not be married more than 6 months, 'cuz people married longer than that don't act like you do.' And then she ran back to her camp."

Yvonne jumped in. "Right then and there, Darren and I promised each other that we'd never be married for longer than 6 months for the rest of our lives!"

It's a great idea, but not always as effortless as it seems to others. "People talk about how marriage takes work," Yvonne added. "Yes, it certainly does, but I don't think it's the kind of work that most people think of. More than taking a lot of time and energy, it's about being mindful. It doesn't take a lot of time or energy to give Darren a 10-second kiss instead of a peck on the cheek, or a 30-second hug instead of a quick pat-pat-pat as I'm running out the door...but it does take some thought."

"And it doesn't take a lot of time or energy for me to call Yvonne from work and say, 'Hey, I'm about to head into a meeting and I've only got a couple of seconds, but I wanted you to know I was thinking about you and I love you!' Or to pick up some flowers from a roadside stand on the way home..."

Yvonne added, "Or better yet, my favorite ice cream..."

Darren laughed. "But we just try to 'think married thoughts' as we go about the day instead of forgetting we're married until we fall into bed at night. Just changing that mindset makes all the difference in the world. When we keep our minds on each other, the time and energy take care of themselves."

It's easy to take people for granted. Oddly enough, that's especially true of the people we love the most. When people think about taking time for each other or working on their relationships, they often feel like that time is another chore on top of an already busy day. Who needs one more thing to squeeze into the schedule? Maybe Darren and Yvonne are onto something, though. Maybe celebrating the fruits of love just means being mindful of love in the moment. Remember that people don't need much—they just need to be noticed. Four-hour date nights, romantic weekends away, and second honeymoons are all wonderful ways to say "I love you," but the real work of any loving relationship is the 30 seconds you take to acknowledge that there is another person in your life—a person you are grateful for, and not an obstacle you have to negotiate around on your way to getting the really important things done.

The work of true love is not about how much energy you invest—it is the willingness to step outside of yourself even for a few moments to say, "You mean the world to me." If you are married, you have already found love: be a blessing to your spouse by taking a few seconds today—literally just a few seconds—to express what a gift you feel he or she is. Think back to that effortless joy and gratitude you felt during the first 6 months of your marriage. If you are not married, think of other beloved people in your life and how joyful you were when you first came to know them. What are ways you can keep those signs of true love alive for the rest of your life?

What Money Can't Buy

The year 2009 was a tough time for Helena and Chuck, 2 former clients. Chuck was laid off midyear from his job at the auto plant, and the couple was barely scraping by on his quickly evaporating unemployment benefits.

Helena and Chuck had 2 kids. Their oldest, Jim, was turning 16 that year. Jim was a good student and loved to play basketball. He was on the varsity squad at his high school. He even held down a regular job at the nursing home, helping the activities coordinator run bingo games, organize trips, and plan special celebrations to make life at the facility more enjoyable for the residents. He could have gotten a job at the fast food place where most of his friends worked, but he said he wanted to do something that would help people. He was a good kid, and his parents were really proud of him.

Helena and Chuck wanted to do something special for Jim's 16th birthday. Before Chuck lost his job, they were planning on buying him a car for his birthday. The family only had one car, and it was an ordeal to get Chuck to work, Jim to work and practice, and Helena to her various errands around town. The plan was that Chuck would use his employee discount to buy a car that was small but safe. If Jim continued to show responsibility around the house, they would give him the car and take him for his permit on his birthday.

Now all that was out of the question. They didn't know what to do for Jim's birthday. There was very little money left for any gift, much less a car. It wasn't that Jim was expecting anything big, but they wanted to do something to show how much they appreciated him.

Not knowing what else to do, Helena and Jim talked together and decided to write Jim a letter. They told him how proud they were of the young man he was becoming. They listed a few of the accomplishments they were most proud of, but mostly they wrote about the little ways that Jim blessed people every day. They talked about his willingness to do chores without being asked twice. They talked about how proud they were that he chose a job that made a difference and didn't just make him money. They talked about how they prayed for him every day and knew that God had great plans for his future, and they each shared some of their favorite memories of his growing up.

When his birthday came, Helena and Chuck were feeling nervous and a little apologetic. They knew Jim understood that there wasn't much to go around that year, but they still wished it could have been more. They gave Jim the letter, and he opened it with a puzzled look on his face.

Now, Jim may have been many things, but like a lot of 16-year-old boys, the one thing he wasn't was talkative. When he finished the letter, he looked up at his mom and dad. They noticed that his eyes were moist. He blinked back a few more tears and hugged them both. "That was the best thing you guys ever gave me. I love you."

Too often we think that saying "I love you" to

someone should be dramatic, with fanfare and expensive and beautifully wrapped packages. But all that drama can distract us from the best gift of all. Find some way to tell people from the bottom of your heart what a difference they have made in your life and what a gift they are to you. By sharing the riches of your love, you'll also discover the depth of true love that others feel for you— no matter how difficult the circumstances.

This Side of Heaven

Like clockwork, the women met for lunch the first Saturday of every month. They had been meeting for 40 years and, God willing, they hoped to keep meeting for many years to come.

They had supported each other through marriage, childbirth, arguments with spouses, divorce, and the raising and launching of children. More and more time these days was spent bragging about grandchildren. In many ways, they had been there for better and worse, for richer and poorer, sickness and health. And now, death had parted them.

A year earlier, Liz, a former colleague of mine and member of this group, had been diagnosed with breast cancer. She didn't tell her friends at first—she didn't want to worry them. But as the situation became clearer and surgery, chemo, and radiation became more imminent, she just couldn't carry on without telling them.

Their group had had minor run-ins with the medical establishment before. Beth's gallstones, Anna's foot surgery, Nicole's face-lift, but as a whole, they were remarkably healthy. They used to joke that with their busy lives, sickness just knew it would have to wait. And it did wait, until it finally made an appointment with Liz.

At first, the small group of friends were Liz's cheerleaders. They helped keep her spirits up through the nausea and the hair loss. After the surgeon told Liz that a mastectomy was absolutely necessary, Nicole brought in a news clipping of a group of boys who had all shaved their heads to support their friend with leukemia. "Aren't we better than a bunch of boys?" she asked. And with the sort of dark humor that could only be appreciated by friends who had been through so much together, she defiantly held up a butter knife and suggested that at their next luncheon, they should all cut off one breast in sympathy. Liz laughed so hard she could barely breathe.

It was just so appallingly inappropriate, so typical of Nicole. Liz said, "Nicole, in your case, it would be a shame to see all that good money go to waste." They all laughed even harder. Because of their closeness and deep understanding of each other's lives, they knew just what to say to pull Liz out of the darkest place she'd ever been.

Later, when the doctor told Liz that the cancer had spread to her liver, she had the wind knocked out of her. After promising that she would come to their next luncheon, she failed to show. She just couldn't face her old friends. The women, however, were not going along with her attempts to pull away. When they realized she wasn't coming, they ordered all the food to go and brought it to Liz's house. When she protested that her house wasn't clean enough and she was too tired, they pushed past her, sat her down in the most comfortable chair, and started cleaning. At first Liz was furious. But her friends were a force to be reckoned with. Eventually she stopped resisting, and her joy at seeing them lessened her depression, at least for one meal. And when the time came for the next luncheon, she made sure to be there.

Later, when she grew too weak to attend any of their

luncheons, her friends returned to her home to tell stories, pray, and sometimes just sit quietly.

Now was the first luncheon since Liz's passing. The group gathered—not so much because they felt like it, but because that's just what they did. They read a letter from Liz's husband thanking them for all they had done. They toasted her memory, and they reflected on how none of them would be who they were without Liz's influence. Anna wouldn't have met her husband if Liz hadn't set them up, back in college. Beth couldn't imagine how she would have made it after her divorce if Liz hadn't put her and her son up for months until she got back on her feet. For Nicole, Liz had been an emotional anchor. When Nicole was going through a serious bout of depression, Liz helped her find a therapist and made sure she made it to each session. She would also "just drop by" with a meal for Nicole's family on the days when Nicole was too emotionally spent to take care of anyone except herself. Each person at the table carried inside of her something Liz had given her, and that gift continued to inspire, challenge, and encourage the women, even now that Liz was no longer with them on this side of heaven.

C.S. Lewis once wrote that "friendship is the least natural of all the loves. It alone has the power to raise us to become gods or angels." At that first luncheon following Liz's passing, Liz's friends reflected on how she had been an angel to them in their lives. They had no doubt that she would continue to be an angel of even more influence now.

Too often we forget how profound friendship can be. People sometimes think of a friend as someone you hang out or pass an idle afternoon with, but not someone as important as a relative or spouse. Close friends, if you are lucky enough to find them, offer a true love that transforms. We are shaped by such friendships. They challenge us to be more than we are and to become everything we were created to be. The true love of our friends, like divine love, lives on—not even death can separate us from these dear ones, if we just allow ourselves to accept their love.

Letting Yourself
Be Loved

We all dream of being loved well, finding someone who
will love each of us for who we are and dedicate his or
her life to being our best friend and partner. But
sometimes, when we get what we want, we don't know
what to do with it.

Jennifer had a painful dating history. She revealed to
me that she'd been with several men who in one way or
another had been abusive or cruel. She'd done a lot of
work on herself to leave those kinds of relationships
behind. Now she was dating Christopher. Christopher
was, according to Jennifer, nearly perfect. He was
successful and handsome. He treated her like a princess.
And she had no idea how to handle it.

"It's like I keep waiting for the other shoe to drop," Jennifer said. "I've never had anyone treat me this well, and I can't just relax and enjoy it. My friends all tell me I'm crazy, but I keep expecting him to disappoint me or hurt me, or start acting like a jerk. On the one hand, it's causing me to overreact to the little things he does that are frustrating—like, if he's late once in a while—and, on the other hand, it stops me from being glad that I'm in a good relationship for a change. Why is it so hard to let myself be loved when it's all I've ever wanted?"

Why, indeed? It can be terrifying to put your heart in someone else's hands. True love is always a risk, and if you have not placed your bets well in the past, you might expect to lose the next time the wheel of love spins around. Learning to trust and open your heart to another takes time, care, and faith. Believe that you can love and be loved.

When I was a child, we had a cherry tree growing in our yard. I used to love to eat the ripe cherries. One year, I couldn't wait for my parents to pick them, and I decided I would pick them myself. I ate an entire lunch bag full of unripe cherries, and I was sick for two days afterward. I developed a hatred of cherries that lasted until adulthood. Many years later, I rediscovered the joys of eating farm-fresh cherries. I could have saved myself a long wait if I'd just accepted that my impatience was to blame for my stomach pains. But the whole unpleasant experience taught me something about love.

If you've been hurt by love before, the trick is to realize that the problem isn't the fruit. It's a matter of timing. You may want to rush to eat unripened fruit because you feel that you can't wait any longer. Or you're afraid you'll miss your chance to eat it at all, and you decide you'd better grab it while you can. But inevitably, this will make you sick.

Pace yourself—exercise patience and faith in the abundance of the world. Learn to recognize what ripe fruit looks like, so that you can enjoy every delicious bite. True love takes time to be found and to come to maturity, but once it is ready to be enjoyed, there is nothing so delicious and sweet.

RU Mine?

Candy hearts. An essential ingredient of puppy love. The NECCO Candy Company began making these little hearts with words back in 1902, with classic messages like KISS ME, BE MINE, and SWEET TALK.

Candymakers continue to come up with sweet new ways to say "I love you." The trick, of course, is saying it concisely. Shakespeare once said "Brevity is the soul of wit." It is apparently the soul of sweet talk, too. These ½-inch hearts can only fit up to 2 words of 4 letters each. Figuring out how to say everything that needs to be said in 8 letters or less is no easy task. Sometimes we can use shortcuts, and sometimes we have to spell it out. U R MINE. EZ 2 LOVE. Candy hearts spoke in the language of text messages before the invention of the cell phone!

Those little candies can have a big impact. With 8 little letters, hearts can be broken—WISE UP!—or set aflutter—URA TIGER.

We can learn a lot from little candy hearts. I once heard a wise person say that we must acknowledge the power of words to create reality. The Book of Genesis says that God spoke the world into being with just a few words. Even human words have tremendous power. Sometimes the smallest words pack the biggest punch. People have incredibly strong reactions to little words like: Love, Hate, God, Hope, Pain, Joy, Lust, and Friend.

Every year the NECCO Candy Company makes 100,000 pounds of candy hearts, enough little words to make a mighty mountain. One hundred thousand pounds might seem like a lot, but the average person says 100,000 words each week (and contrary to the myth, both men and women say about the same number of words—16,000 each day). Our words are like candy hearts we heap on those around us. Every day we get to decide whether to suffocate them with anger or disdain, or shower them with grace, peace, and love. And the words we speak can make lifelong impressions. When you seek to love truly, you'll choose your words carefully. What words is your heart speaking today? Find room in your heart to write LOVE 4U so that others may write that to you as well.

Open Yourself
to Love
Everywhere

When in Rome...

Everyone talks about finding true love, but how many people understand what true love really is. Is it a feeling? A wish? Many people tell me they've heard that love is a decision—but a decision to do what?

This question is raised in the movie *When in Rome*. The film tells the story of a young woman (Kristen Bell) who, after being traumatized by the news that her boyfriend is engaged to another woman, must travel to Rome to be a bridesmaid in her friend's wedding. After initiating a series of unfortunate events that nearly destroy the reception, she gets hopelessly drunk. In her misery she decides to steal four coins from the renowned Fontana D'Amore (Fountain of Love). Her intentions are good— she is trying to save people who still expect their wishes for true love to come true. She doesn't know, however, that according to an ancient myth, anyone who takes a coin from the fountain will magically and irresistibly capture the heart of the person who tossed the coin into the fountain in the first place.

The myth turns out to be true, and the owners of the four coins pursue her, in increasingly odd ways. Danny DeVito, the middle-aged "Sausage King," fills her office with gift baskets of his best links. Jon Hader, a street magician, breaks into her apartment and unsuccessfully attempts to perform an escape in her honor while bound and hanging upside down from her ceiling. Starving artist Will Arnett paints a nude portrait of her on the side of a building in her neighborhood, and Dax Shepard, a narcissistic male model, tries to impress her by displaying his rock-hard abs and his creepy ability to show up in a matching outfit wherever she is, regardless of the occasion.

Of course, she doesn't love any of them (and they don't really love her, either—they are under a spell). She's in love with another man altogether. Despite the silliness, though, there's a poignant moment when the four suitors finally realize that she's genuinely in love with someone else. Their initial impulse, of course, is to sabotage her efforts to win his heart. The Sausage King stops them cold when he says, "We say that we love her. When you love someone, you have to put their needs before your own."

Putting another's needs before our own doesn't come easily, but it is a powerful definition of true love. It's always so much easier to manipulate a situation so that it suits our own purposes, or to treat another person as a means to an end. But true love helps us reach down deep and find the courage to do the least natural thing in the world: to let someone else's deepest needs outweigh our own, even if it means "losing" them.

Who will you put first today? Whose needs can you put above your own today? A coworker you dislike? Your spouse? A friend? Any time you choose to make a sacrifice, whether great or small, you make a decision to love truly.

Family Footprints

The picnic area was overrun with casseroles, pasta salad, platters of grilled hot dogs and hamburgers and kielbasas, and bowls of various chips and dips. Adults were playing horseshoes, and kids were playing tag and pelting each other with water balloons filled at the spigot by the picnic shelter.

It was the Jankoskis' annual family reunion. Kids, grandkids, uncles, aunts, cousins, in-laws, and a few honorary relatives all gathered together to reconnect, catch up, remember, and dream about the future.

Families come in all sizes, shapes, and colors, but whether yours is over 100 people strong, like the Jankoskis, or just a few people, all strong families have something in common: they give a group of people a place to call home, a place where they can say "I belong here." Even if personalities sometimes clash, the foods, games, inside jokes, rituals, familiar faces, and shared traditions make family feel like a home you can go back to again and again.

Think about your own relatives. If you look back and remember a family gathering, it's remarkable to consider that you witnessed the manifestation of love. Love took shape and was playing and laughing right before your eyes. Amazing, isn't it? After all, you can't see love. You can't taste it, touch it, smell it, or hold it in your hand. But it is real, and it has real power to create something remarkable—a family. One day, there is nothing. Then there is a little spark between two people. Then a child is born. And another. And perhaps another. And soon there is an entire community of people with titles like mom and dad, sister and brother, grandma and grandpa, aunt and uncle.

It's easy to focus so much on the individuality of each person that we forget something essential: all these individuals, different though they may be, belong to a community. They were all brought into being and drawn into communion by the love that bears their family name. Family has the power to take something invisible and make it visible: the strength of the love that creates and sustains.

This visible love, especially the love within a family, is not always joyful and peaceful. It can be messy, loud, intrusive, and exhausting. Especially if you are from a large family, there may be times when you wish you could run far away from the noise and craziness of your relations. But imagine life without family and how much richer your life can be with people who share so much of your history and memories.

A woman I once knew was a compulsive neat-freak. She felt compelled to have everything just so, to the point that when she was cleaning her house she would try to make all the vacuum lines on the carpet parallel to each other. It used to infuriate her when, after a period of compulsive vacuuming, her husband or one of her children would step on the carpet and break the lines or leave the first footprint. Although she loved and cherished her husband and kids, she was beginning to see her family as an intrusion on her life. One day I had her imagine that her carpet was perfectly smooth, that the lines were perfectly parallel and the carpet was footprint-free. In that moment she looked relaxed, serene, and almost blissful. Then I invited her to go further.

"Now as you look at the perfectly clean carpet in the perfectly clean room, I want you to realize that the reason the room is so perfect is that no one else is there. Your family is gone, and they are never coming back. You are alone in your perfectly clean house, standing on your perfectly clean parallel-lined carpet, and you will continue to be alone tomorrow and the next day and the next, until the day you die."

She didn't feel so peaceful anymore. But she got the message. The presence of others—especially family—is much more of a blessing than a challenge. To find true love, you have to step out of your comfort zone and give up your need to have things be "just so" in your life. Sooner or later, someone is going to leave a footprint. But in return for the mess, you get to experience the warm embrace of people who remind you where you come from and where you are going—people who remind you that you are truly loved.

God's Gift to the World

A song (to the tune of Beethoven's *Hymn to Joy*)

> *Joyful, Joyful, I adore me.*
> *I'm the greatest guy on earth!*
> *Hearts unfold like flowers before me.*
> *Earth rejoices at my birth.*
> *And the sun, in all its glory,*
> *rises and sets upon my rear.*
> *So I sally forth in splendor,*
> *spreading joy and spreading cheer!*

(Key Change for Dramatic Emphasis)

> *Joyful, Joyful, I adore me. Sing a song of self-*
> *esteem. Some folks, well, were just more equal.*
> *You are skim milk. I am cream.*
> *Banish thoughts of imperfection.*
> *No more false hu-mi-li-ty.*
> *Have you ever, in your lifetime,*
> *met someone as grand as me?*

When someone says that you think you're God's gift to the world, it's usually not a compliment.

We all know someone who thinks a bit too much of himself—the kind of person who believes he deserves to be praised just for breathing. Many of us also know from experience that such a person is virtually incapable of finding true love because there's no room in his heart for anyone but himself.

But there's a completely different way of thinking of this phrase. Any time you commit an act of true love, you really *are* God's gift to the world.

C.S. Lewis writes that just as a mother helps a child when he is first learning to form his letters, God holds our hands while we learn to love. You are God's gift to the world, and He guides you while you learn day by day what it takes to become a more wonderful gift. Everything about you was created to work for the good of others. Your gifts—our talents, your experiences, even your body—was given to you so that you can use them as a blessing to yourself and others.

Our culture isn't used to thinking of our gifts, talents, experiences, and selves this way. We live in a society of *me* and *mine*. People think, "My talents are given to me for my enjoyment, my experiences are there for my nostalgia, and my body is mine to do with as I please." But true love allows you to see beyond this me-centered culture and empowers you to create a culture of love, where you treat others with dignity, respect, and generosity.

"But what about me?" you might say. If you are so concerned with being a gift to others, are you in danger of losing yourself? While it is possible not to take care of your own needs, true love never means giving yourself to someone who does not respect you. If love is healthy and true, it will be given and received with joy and respect. At the same time, once you've made a commitment to love, true love will show you how to hold nothing back.

You find yourself not by holding yourself apart but by making a sincere gift of yourself. Use your gifts, talents, experiences, and your very self to make someone else's life easier or more pleasant. The more you do this, the more you will come to see your value reflected in the way you are treasured, valued, celebrated, and protected by the people you give yourself to. You really do become God's gift!

On a recent reality TV show about the struggle to overcome addiction, a young woman was in family therapy to overcome her addiction to cocaine. She was dying. The therapist made it clear that in large part, she was doing it to get her father's attention and affirmation. The woman's father, who was present at the therapy session, remained distant and cold, and he received this revelation in a way that sent chills up my spine. I'm not changing, he said. "No one ever changed anything for me, and I'm not changing for her."

In this difficult situation, it's no surprise that she acted out. It's part of our very nature to crave love and to wither away when we don't get it. Even babies do this. When babies are born, if they don't receive love and affection they develop a condition called "failure to thrive." Unless they know first of all that they are loved, they will even refuse food, and allow themselves to waste away. What a tragedy!

The most basic human need is to love and be loved. Of course, all of us are sometimes tempted to hold back. We're afraid of so many things: being hurt, begin taken advantage of, being seen as foolish. But every time we give in to those fears and hold back, avoiding vulnerability, we surrender a little bit of our humanity. Over time, being afraid of surrender can cause us to surrender far too much.

What are you holding back in your life right now? Why are you holding back? And what will show you that it's safe to open yourself to the True Love that casts out your fear? What will it take to let yourself be God's gift, the gift to others that God has made you to be?

Sorry, Charlie

"It took me 25 years to realize I wasn't going to get any credit for giving my wife stuff she didn't want." Charlie sat in my office looking chagrined. It was his last session in a successful series of marriage counseling meetings between him and his wife, Liz, and I'd asked Charlie to describe the one lesson that stuck out for him about the whole experience. I knew that his answer was sincere, and that the realization hadn't come easily.

Charlie and Liz met at college and got married shortly after graduation. They had 3 kids together. Charlie threw himself into work. "Part of me felt a lot of pressure to provide. I was terrified that I would let Liz and the kids down. But another part of me loved the work. I figured out I was good at it. I found my niche, and I parked myself in it."

Charlie became successful and enjoyed the rewards of

his efforts. His family wanted for little. He built a big house, the family went on great vacations and, by all outward appearances, they had a great life.

The problem was, Liz and the kids were lonely. They wanted Charlie, not just his paycheck. "I was always grateful for how hard Charlie worked," Liz said, "and we certainly all enjoyed the money, but he spent so many hours at the office. He missed so much of the kids' lives. For most of our marriage I felt like a single mom."

Charlie used to get defensive when Liz would complain. "I told her she was never happy. I'd say I was working my tail off to give her and the kids a good life, and I accused her of not appreciating anything I did for her. It took all this" (Charlie gestured toward me and the office) "to get me to realize I was giving her what I wanted to give her, not what she needed me to give her."

"It wasn't as if I didn't appreciate everything Charlie did. I just wanted more of *him*."

"I guess I didn't get that." He looked at Liz, "but now I do. It's going to be different from now on."

As children, because we are not capable of doing more, the gift is about the effort: the time we spent painting and

stringing the macaroni necklace, the effort that went into the dandelion bouquet, and the fact that we were willing to spend our allowance on the chipped ceramic elephant we purchased at our grade school's Santa's Workshop sale. In gift-giving it is the thought that counts, but as our capacity for more complex thought develops, gift-giving should also involve more complexity. At some point, it's no longer enough to think merely of some gift. For the thought to genuinely count, we have to *think of the person* to whom we are giving the gift. What does he want from us? What does she need?

You've probably heard the story of the little boy who gives his mom a baseball for her birthday because that's what he wants. Are you ever like that little boy? It's much easier to give people stuff that they don't want—stuff that's easier for you to give than what they really want or need—and then pat yourself on the back for what you think is your generosity.

Gifts given for the sake of true love seek to serve the heart of the recipient. When you give someone what you want to give, you emphasize your own specialness. But when you give someone what they need, you emphasize their specialness to you. The whole point of giving a gift is to thank someone for being a gift to you.

Sometimes you may be afraid to ask people what they really want from you because they might tell you. In responding, you might have to leave your comfort zone behind. You might have to learn new things. You might have to tread uncertain paths. But that is what makes finding true love an adventure. True love should turn you upside down, shake you, and leave you wondering which end is up. It should make you question the very things you thought you knew best about yourself and inspire you to be more than what you are in this moment.

When you prepare to give a gift from true love, all of this happens. Genuine gifts come from real consideration. You have to take time to get to know the recipient. You have to reflect on the way that the other person is a gift to you, so that you can honor that person's gifts with your own.

Today, give people a gift they really want. Let it reflect your time, yourself, and your understanding of who they really are. Show them love, and be willing to let that love transform yourself as well.

The Velveteen Rabbit

Some people want to stay exactly as they are. Never changing. Never changed.

Robert was that way. Sitting across the room from me with his arms folded, he made it clear that he was in marriage counseling under protest. "Look, she knew who I was when she married me. What you see is what you get. Now she wants me to change. I don't think that's fair. I'm happy—why can't she be happy?"

Gina looked like she was ready to burst. "I don't *want* you to change. Our life *needs* you to change. When I met you, we didn't have three kids, a mortgage, and this life we created together! It was fine for us to be who we were back then, but now things are different because we made them different. Now we have to be different. The only reason you're happy is because I'm busy accommodating your fantasy that nothing's changed since we were dating. You're the only one not being pulled in a million directions. I. Can't. Take it. Anymore."

Gina has a point. Most of us would love nothing more than to be affirmed in our okay-ness, to be told that we never have to grow or change again because we're just fine exactly the way we already are. Unfortunately, that's just not the way life is.

It's a basic fact of evolution. When life changes, those who change with it live and grow and flourish. Whether it's boyfriends and girlfriends, colleagues, friends and family, or even people we have just met, relationships change us because they change the circumstances of our life. We are never the same people coming into relationships as we are going out of them.

In the classic children's tale, *The Velveteen Rabbit* by Margery Williams, a plush rabbit becomes a young boy's favorite toy. The rabbit is even more cherished than all the shiny toys who think they are real because they have mechanical parts. The boy takes the rabbit everywhere and does everything with this constant companion. The more time he spends with the boy, the more the rabbit begins to change. Slowly, the shiny velveteen fur wears off, and the bunny becomes threadbare and shabby. But the changes in his physical appearance give no hint of the deeper changes going on inside the rabbit.

Later, the boy becomes sick with scarlet fever. The doctor orders all the child's things burned and sends the boy to recover at seaside. All the toys—the mechanical toys, the velveteen rabbit and others—are placed in a fiery heap. But at the last moment, the velveteen rabbit is saved. The Nursery Fairy is able to help the rabbit escape because the boy's love has made him real. The rabbit finds a home in the woods as the other toys, unused and unloved, perish in the fire.

Love can pull us in all sorts of directions we'd rather not be pulled. It can challenge us and stretch us. There is no question that it will change us. Ultimately, it will make us real. Love can cause pain, but it is the only thing that can save us.

Each of us has a choice to make. Like Gina's husband, we can choose to fool ourselves and be like the toys that thought they were real because they had moving parts. We can lapse into mechanical habits that suit no one but ourselves, and sit idle and lonely like toys on a shelf. Or we can do the work of love. We can allow our fur to be rubbed off giving hugs. We can become a little threadbare for the sake of caring for another. We can make sacrifices to our comforts as love changes us and makes us real. And we can live forever.

Today, and every day, choose well. Choose to grow in whatever direction life is calling you to grow. This is the path to true love.

Unexpected Blessings

When Catelin and Randy's daughter Linda was born with Down's syndrome, they were devastated, but as they sat with me years later, they had a very different attitude.

"It's weird," said Catelin. "You go through so many feelings when you find out your child has Down's. Of course, you love your child, but you also feel devastated and depressed, and guilty for feeling devastated and depressed. People don't know what to say. You can get offended if they try to sympathize with you. 'Don't be sad for me. This is my baby!' And you can get angry if they try to be cheerful about it—either because it can come off as fake or because you think, 'You have no idea how I'm feeling inside.'"

Randy agreed. "When you're becoming a parent, everyone starts imagining what it's going to be like. The things you're going to do with your kid. How it's going to be. It takes a while to adjust all those fantasies."

"The funny thing," said Catelin, "is that you have to 'let go' of a lot fewer of those dreams for your child than you think you will. Linda loves school. She's doing great in Special Olympics. She loves playing with Fluffy, our dog."

As Catelin and Randy have reflected on their life since Linda was born, they've come to some remarkable insights. As Randy puts it, "A long time ago, I heard someone say, 'God gives you the children you need.' If someone had said that to me when Linda was born, I think I would have punched them. I would have thought, 'Are you saying God needed to send me a broken child to fix something that was wrong with me?' But now I see what that saying means. Linda's not broken. She's just Linda. And she's pretty wonderful. And, yeah, she's exactly what Catelin and I needed.'

Catelin added, "It might sound strange to people who don't have a child with special needs, but we don't really see her as disabled. Every kid is different in some way.

Some kids have blue eyes, some brown. Some kids are geniuses, some kids struggle. Some kids are great at sports, others are better at music. Some are tall, some are short. And some have Down's. It's true that Randy and I struggled with that at first, but it isn't something Linda struggles with. She's fine with who she is. She's just the greatest kid. We love her to death.

But what about the special care that a child with Down's requires? Special schools, worries about medical issues, teasing from other kids, emotional struggles? Doesn't it all pile up sometimes?

"Look," says Randy, "I don't know a parent in the world who isn't run a little ragged by their kid's school and activities schedule. All parents worry about their child getting teased or sick. We're no different. That's just parenting. But in the same way, parenting, for any parent, isn't just work. It's a lot of fun, too."

Catelin adds, "I guess what we're saying is that it's not like we're burning ourselves out taking care of Linda 24/7. Or that we're saints because we have a Down's child. People don't understand how much Linda gives back to us. I wasn't sure I'd ever be able to say this when she was first diagnosed, but she's really an amazing kid."

"Sometimes," says Randy, "I'll look at other families and see how they're bickering, or hear about problems that they're having with their kids, and it just makes me pull Linda a little closer and thank God she's ours. It sounds like a cliché, but blessings really can come in unexpected packages. I know Linda sure did. We're glad she's our blessing."

True love can change us in unexpected ways. Especially when we receive the blessings that come instead of trying to find a different kind of blessing. Our lives are filled with little opportunities to love that challenge us to grow in directions that we might not have chosen for ourselves, but love is like that. Love knows our hearts—and what our hearts need to grow—better than we do.

Discover Love
in Every Person

I'm Here for You

Most of us would like to believe we are self-sufficient. We don't want to be a burden to others. We want to take care of ourselves. Finding true love means understanding that all of us are connected and draw strength from one another.

Bethany was a proud, single mom of Jared, a 13-year-old boy. Her ex-husband, Matt, was completely out of the picture. He'd become an alcoholic after they got married and then dropped out of life: first he left the marriage, then his job, then his last known address. Bethany didn't know how to begin to find him. To make up for the lack of child support, she started working two jobs.

It was hard to keep her head above water, but Bethany was making it—until Jared was diagnosed with osteosarcoma of the leg, a kind of bone cancer that affects teens. Historically, amputation was a common way to prevent the cancer from spreading throughout the body, but today chemotherapy and limb—salvage surgery (replacing the diseased bone with bone grafts) can give people about an 80% chance of surviving. Nevertheless, the treatment is arduous, exhausting, and expensive. Thankfully, Bethany's employers were as accommodating as they could be, but the work still needed to get done, and she couldn't be in two places at once.

"There was one morning when my replacement at work called in sick, so my shift wasn't covered. I couldn't reschedule Jared's chemo because the doctor was going to be on vacation. I broke down. I kept trying to figure out how I was going to make it all happen. I hate asking for help. I can't stand when people pity me because I'm a single mom—like it' s some kind of disease—but that morning I just lost it. I didn't know what to do." She was crying—sobbing, really—when the phone rang. It was Meghan, a new friend from church, just calling to catch up. "Normally, I just make small talk. I have a hard time opening up to people, especially after everything with Matt, but I couldn't hold back. She said, 'How are you?' and it was like a bomb went off at the base of the dam holding everything back. I spilled my guts to her."

Meghan listened, and when Bethany came up for air, she told Bethany to go to work. She would be more than happy to take Jared to his treatment, keep Bethany posted the entire time, and after treatment, have Jared stay with her at her house until Bethany could finish her shift. Bethany tried to refuse, but Meghan was calling from her cell phone, and as soon as she heard Bethany start to explain what was going on, she interrupted her errands and started driving straight to Bethany's place. As they finished the conversation, Meghan was ringing Bethany's doorbell!

"I'm here for you," Meghan said. It was the first of many times Meghan would be there throughout Jared's recovery.

"I couldn't have gotten through all this without her," Bethany recalled to me some time later. "I feel like she saved our lives. Obviously, she was an angel to Jared, but the whole experience taught me to be willing to open my heart again. When I met Matt, I didn't have any boundaries up. I trusted everybody. And when he left me, I shut myself off. My friendship with Meghan taught me that I could risk needing people again."

Jared today is a healthy 17-year-old, and Bethany is engaged to Michael, a man she truly feels cherishes her. "I know there's no way I'd ever have been willing to go out with Michael, much less marry him, if hadn't had to accept Meghan's help. That whole process helped me get over myself, lose my pride, and open my heart to people.

"It sounds childish, but I always tease Meghan that she's my BFF because she really is one of those friends you can count on to be there for you no matter what. And that's something worth celebrating."

True love is always worth celebrating, and the best form of celebration is to open yourself to it. Who is offering you friendship and help today? Are you ready to accept it, and are you ready to offer it to others so that they too can find true love, even if they do not know how to ask for it?

21,535
First Dates

In the film *50 First Dates*, Henry Roth (Adam Sandler) falls in love with Lucy Whitmore (Drew Barrymore) who, due to an automobile accident, has an extremely severe case of short-term memory loss. She can recall who she is from day to day, but every morning when she wakes up, she is convinced that it is her father's birthday—the day of the accident. She has no recollection of the year that has passed in the interim. To shield her from the pain of being told about her accident every day, her father and brother play along and pretend that each new day is her father's birthday.

Henry meets Lucy at a café and becomes completely smitten with her. He eventually goes through the process of winning Lucy's heart every day, trying to take the courtship a little further each time, despite having to start every morning with a new introduction.

Although the disorder that caused Lucy's memory loss was a convenient fiction for the film, in a sense, each of us introduces ourselves anew each day to the people we love. Who will I be today? Will I be the loving, supportive spouse, the sensitive parent, the caring friend? Perhaps I'll be the busy, overwhelmed partner, the harried parent, or the self-absorbed friend. Or maybe I'll be the resentful spouse, the reactive parent, and the rejecting friend.

We like to think that we get credit for who we were yesterday or the day before, but in truth, our credit is quickly overextended, and the memories of our past dedication fade rapidly if we forget to reintroduce ourselves every day to those we love, as a person who can be counted upon to love, care, and support them.

Some people are intimidated by this reality. They grow resentful that they can't just coast on their past loving accomplishments. They treat relationships as a race that can be run and won, after which they can retire and bask in the glow of their early victory. I meet far too many husbands who aren't completely joking when they say

that "marriage means never having to buy flowers again."
And too many friends complain "she doesn't give me any
credit!"

But those who are well-versed in finding true love
know that every day, in fact every moment, is another
opportunity to introduce ourselves to the people in our
life. Who will you be? Someone who cares and will go to
great lengths to demonstrate your concern, or someone
who won't lift a finger to help? Every moment is pregnant
with loving purpose, and you can set yourself to the task
of loving, even if this sometimes means covering territory
that's been covered before and finding a way to move
forward from that point.

Odds are you'll have 59 years as an adult. So as an
adult, you'll have 21,535 first dates with the people who
share your life. Every day, the introductions start again.
Today, when you introduce yourself to the people you
love, who will you be?

No Greater Love

Walt Kowalski, played by Clint Eastwood in the movie *Gran Torino*, is an angry man. He is estranged from his adult children, friendless, hostile to his priest and his neighbors, alone, and happy to be left that way. A veteran of the Korean War, Walt is decidedly unhappy when a Hmong family, the Vang Lors, moves in next door to him in his poor working-class neighborhood in Detroit.

The Vang Lors' son, Thao, is being tormented by a gang. Thao knows that if he doesn't join with the gang members they'll destroy him, so he decides to sign up. As part of the initiation, the gang leader orders Thao to steal Walt's prized 1972 Gran Torino. The reluctant theft fails, and Thao is required to work for Walt to pay off this debt to him.

A friendship grows between Walt and the Lor family. Walt finds himself beginning to care about the boy in spite of himself. He takes on the role of protector and counselor to the teenager. The grumpy curmudgeon eventually helps the boy land a job and even gives Thao advice on love.

After the gang escalates its violence toward the Lor family, Walt threatens the leader at gunpoint in an attempt to warn them off. The gang responds with a violent and devastating attack against the Lor family. Thao desperately asks for Walt's help exacting revenge, but after agreeing, Walt tricks Thao and traps him in his basement so that Walt can confront the gang leader alone. Walt, a man who once seemed to care for no one but himself, begins taking steps that will put his life on the line for the love of others.

In the dramatic conclusion, Walt sets up a situation where he, in essence, sacrifices his life for the Vang Lors. We think he is going to fight. We expect Clint Eastwood to reprise his role as Dirty Harry and take out the gang in a bloody denouement. But Walt has a different idea. He simply asks the gang to stop persecuting the Vang Lors. During the resulting pause, Walt reaches into his pocket. Everyone thinks he is going for a gun. Walt is struck down in a hail of gunfire and in the presence of a number of witnesses.

Later, we discover that the unarmed Walt was simply reaching for the lighter to light the cigarette dangling from his lips. The gang members mistook his actions and murdered him in cold blood. They are arrested and jailed. "Greater love has no man than to lay down his life for his friend," says the oft-quoted John 15:13. The Vang Lors are safe because of Walt's sacrifice.

Love has a way of changing even those who are sure they don't care about love. To paraphrase the memorable words of the poet Francis Thompson, we flee love "down the nights and down the days, down the arches of the years and down the labyrinthine ways of our own mind." When we give up our isolation and self-protection, we are freed to become connected and involved with those in our lives. The power of that connection opens the way for a love that can change us and the lives of those around us for the better.

Isn't She Lovely?

Keira had been nervous when she was pregnant. "I was so excited about the baby coming, but I had no idea what I was doing. I was an only child. I'd never been around little kids, much less babies, and I felt so intimidated at the prospect."

Her husband, Len, wasn't much more confident, "I was excited, but terrified. I was pretty sure I'd break the baby somehow. I had no idea what having a baby would be like. I was sure I would be the most incompetent dad ever."

But things changed once baby Nicole was born. "Things just sort of fell into place," Keira recalled. "We still have a lot to learn as parents but, I mean, the first time they placed Nicole in my arms, I just knew it was going to be okay. She latched on to me, and I nuzzled her head under my chin, and it just felt right."

Len has similar feelings. "I remember sitting on the side of the hospital bed, looking at K and Nicole and thinking to myself, 'This is good. This is really good.' I didn't know what else to think or say. I just knew that I wasn't afraid. Somehow, we were going to work it all out together."

There is something about the joy of new life that opens doors, reveals possibilities, and frees us to discover love like we've never experienced it before. Having children expands and changes us. American writer Peter De Vries wrote, "The value of marriage is not that adults produce children but that children produce adults." We can never be prepared *in advance* to be wonderful parents—we have to take the leap, knowing that somehow, with love, it really does work out. We grow so that they can grow.

If love is the decision to work for the good of someone else without counting the cost, then raising children is a perfect example of the gift of love. We invest so much of ourselves into our children, and there are so few guarantees. But the one thing we can guarantee is that loving children will demand more from us, and give back more to us, than almost any other endeavor. As parents, my wife and I have discovered this countless times, just as other parents have done.

To be afraid of having children is to be afraid of love. What could be more amazing, more desirable, than 2 people sharing a love so powerful that in 9 months it has to be given its own name? The power to take love, something you can't see, and make it visible by giving that love real life, should be celebrated.

After the birth of his first child, Aisha, in 1975, Stevie Wonder penned a song *Isn't She Lovely* that's still popular today. "I never thought through love we'd be / Making one as lovely as she / But isn't she lovely made from love."

The truth of this song is always surprising. Every one of us has been made *from* love and *for* love. You can celebrate the gift of your own life by loving someone today. And if you have a child, or are close to a child, let that little one know how precious he or she is in your eyes. Let them be the face of true love in your life today.

In Giving Love, You Find It

Karen's father had an inoperable brain tumor, and he was slowly dying. For several weeks now, he had been unable to move or speak. Karen spent most days at his bedside feeding him ice chips to help him stay hydrated and comfortable, and talking to him, though he gave no sign that he was aware of her presence.

"Some people think I'm a little bit crazy. They'd understand if I visited for a little while, y'know, did the dutiful daughter thing, came and went. But they wonder why I'm here all day with him when it's obvious that he gets so little from my visits. They tend to think—and I know this because Dad's medical social worker told me as much—that I must have some kind of unresolved daddy issues I'm trying to work out, or that I'm deluding myself into thinking he's aware of what I'm doing for him and hoping he'll wake up and pat me on the head. But neither of those things have anything to do with it."

Karen explained that she stays there for two main reasons. "The first thing I'm doing is trying to stand up for Dad's dignity. They're really busy on this floor, and some patient is always calling out for this and pressing the nurse's call button for that. They do take care of him, but I need to be here to ask them for little things like an extra pillow to prop him up or an extra blanket if he gets goose pimples. Without me to advocate for him, I think it would be very easy for people to forget that he was here.

"But there's something else they don't get. Growing up, Dad was always there for me. Getting to be here for him now is really special. Sure, it's hard to see him like this, but even now I feel like he's giving something back to me. He's helping me be a better person. Dad was the one, even more than mom, who used to talk to me about virtues and faith and that, no matter what, a person deserved to be treated with a little dignity. What I didn't appreciate was how much somebody in Dad's condition could give back just by giving me a chance to take care of him.

"I've always struggled with being a little bit of a selfish

person. I was usually thinking, 'What's in it for me?' There aren't a lot of places in my life where I do something without getting anything back at all. This is the first time I'm getting a chance to do something purely selfless. It's funny how good that feels. Dad was always teaching me something. Even now, he's still showing me that I have a lot to learn."

We've all heard that it's better to give than to receive, but until we have an opportunity like Karen's, it's difficult to understand how that can be true. Giving without counting the cost is an important part of finding true love. In a world where we scrutinize every situation to make sure it provides an adequate payoff, giving freely is a tremendous relief. We find that the rewards are greater than we could imagine.

Everyone has opportunities large and small every day to practice this kind of giving. Who needs a little bit more from you today? What can you do to make their lives easier or more pleasant without expecting anything back? Resolve today to give freely. You might be surprised to discover what you receive in return.

Your Life Is the Greatest Love Story Ever Told

We were created for love.

Every cell in our body craves love. We simply cannot live without it. As we saw, infants will refuse food if they are not loved. Adults become isolated and depressed, and ultimately ill if they are not loved. Of all groups, it is happily married people who are healthier and live longer than anyone else. Love is the source and summit of our being.

Many people believe they can live without love. They pride themselves on their rugged individualism, their strength, and their autonomy. But their lives, filled with accomplishments though they may be, are impoverished without love. In the immortal words of St. Paul:

If I speak in the tongues of men and of angels, but have not love, I am only a resounding gong or a clanging cymbal. If I have the gift of prophecy and can fathom all mysteries and all knowledge, and if I have a faith that can move mountains, but have not love, I am nothing. If I give all I possess to the poor and surrender my body to the flames, but have not love, I gain nothing. (1 Cor 13:13)

In this life or the next, our success is not measured by the greatness of our deeds, but by the greatness of our hearts. The challenge for each of us is to leave our hearts open to finding and giving true love despite our fears and vulnerability.

Love hurts. Sometimes the pain of love comes from the challenges we face in being stretched in directions that we would rather not be stretched. As children, many of us experienced growing pains as our bones, muscles, and sinews reached to fulfill their potential. But the pain we felt in our physical growth dwarfs the pain we encounter as we are challenged to grow emotionally. The temptation to shut down our hearts can be very strong.

But as much as true love hurts, it can also heal. It can nourish even more. The heart that is rooted in love is a happy heart; the person who resists the temptation to wall off her heart and instead embraces every opportunity to love even more is a person primed to lead a rich, full life.

The Positive Psychology movement studies what it takes to live a full and satisfied life. These psychologists tell us that intimacy is one key to authentic happiness, as is the ability to remain hopeful, resilient, and even joyful in light of the ups and downs of everyday life. People want to be happy, but they tend to pursue happiness in ways that will lead to anything but happiness.

Most people think that it's enough to seek pleasure, or enjoyment, or the mere absence of conflict. But psychologists, theologians, and philosophers agree that these things tend not to last. People who exhibit authentic happiness know how to enjoy themselves. They engage in many pleasurable pursuits and know when to avoid conflict (as well as when to instigate it). But beyond this, those who make authentic happiness their goal look for every opportunity to love more, to love better, and to make all of their intimate relationships healthier and deeper.

Many love stories end with "and they lived happily ever after." We all want our own happy ending. And in fact, you can have it. Your life could be the greatest love story ever told.

In every great love story there is a quest to find true love, an undying commitment to fulfill the mission, obstacles that must be overcome, and dragons that must be slain. You may think that your love story lacks such dramatic elements, but I can guarantee, and you know from your own experience, that your love story has both harrowing and heroic moments.

I believe that on the day we are born, each of us is sent on a quest to find true love and claim the hearts of as many people as we can. Along the way, we must conquer the tremendous obstacles in our own heart: fear, our own limitations, and self-defeating tendencies. We also must vanquish many dragons: selfishness, pride, addictions to our own comforts, and a terror of vulnerability. The journey can be intimidating at times, but we come well-equipped with a weapon that is more than up to the task—the giving of ourselves.

The giving of ourselves (or self-donation) is the most powerful form of love. It alone can help us find the true meaning of our lives and give us the power to overcome any obstacle in our path. Self-donation is a kind of heroic generosity that allows us to think of our whole self—our gifts, talents, experiences, and even our own bodies—as a gift that has been given to us by God to work for the good of others. To wield this powerful weapon is to acknowledge that there is no obstacle that cannot be overcome, no dragon that cannot be vanquished. For love is stronger than death."

Every interaction with your partner, children, family, friends, and coworkers represents a chance to write another chapter in your love story. Every time you encounter another person, an invitation to love is extended to you. Every time you choose to respond to that invitation, to extend yourself in some way—great or small—to work for the good of the other, your heart grows and your love story becomes more compelling, more grace-filled, and more heroic.

You may not think of yourself as a hero, but there is

nothing more heroic than choosing to seek and to offer true love. A hero does what is difficult. Against the odds, he conquers himself and the challenges that stand between him and fulfillment of his quest. If he finds his happy-ever-after, it is only because he was dauntless in his pursuit of love and faithful in his finding, no matter what the cost.

When you choose to love, really love. Don't let anything, especially your own personal preferences, comforts, or limitations stand in the way. You are living a hero's life—you are writing a love story that will be told throughout time and be a blessing for generations to come.

My prayer for you is that your quest to find true love will transform your life into the greatest love story ever told.

Discover the Wisdom of Dr. Popcak

Dr. Gregory K. Popcak is a trusted guide for those who seek to deepen their relationships with others. The primary focus of his work is to help married couples grow stronger together using the wisdom of both psychology and faith. In books such as *Holy Sex!* and *A Marriage Made for Heaven*, Dr. Greg shows you how to build a marriage that celebrates your partner as a gift from God. *Holy Sex!* helps us overcome the idea that Catholicism has a negative view of intimacy. He shows how the Church affirms intimacy in many forms, as an expression of love and a vehicle for life. *A Marriage Made for Heaven* applies these insights and others in a format appropriate for parishes wanting to create marriage enrichment programs for their members.

Of course, sometimes it can seem like the Catholic idea of love is too abstract and saintly—for someone else but not for us. That's why Dr. Greg offers us *God Help Me! These People Are Driving Me Nuts* and *God Help Me! This Stress Is Driving Me Crazy*. These two books speak frankly about real-life frustrations Dr. Greg sees in the people he counsels and in his own life as well as practical ways to work through those frustrations in a way that honors God's will for our lives. Like the stories in *How to Find True Love*, both books show us that the way to a deeper life is not by avoiding what troubles us but by learning to identify it and find tools to deal with it.

Finally, there are times when the challenges we face go even deeper than individuals or specific sources of stress, and we feel that nothing is working. At these moments when we come to a crossroad, God may be inviting us to a totally different way of living. *In The Life God Wants You to Have: Discovering the Divine Plan When Human Plans Fail*, Dr. Greg walks us through real-life stories of people who have faced financial ruin, health disasters, and marriage melt-downs, yet through diligence have learned to hear God leading them to a more faith-filled place. Whatever your own situation in life, invite Dr. Greg's wisdom into your daily path, as he guides you through decisions small and large. Order the books mentioned here, and if you wish, learn more about Dr. Greg at www.exceptionalmarriages.com.

Other Works by the Author
GREGORY K. POPCAK, PH.D.

HOLY SEX!
A Catholic Guide to Toe-Curling, Mind-Blowing,
Infallible Loving

"Think of this book as Thomas Aquinas meets Dr. Ruth and enjoy!"
–John Allen, Jr.

Holy Sex! unveils Christianity's best-kept secret, and does so in an informative, solidly grounded, and delightful way. Want to know your *Holy Sex Quotient*? Ever wondered why Catholics have better sex more often? From a presentation of the Church's actual teachings on sex to "The Infallible Lover's Guide to Pleasure" to "Natural Family Planning" to a Q&A section on "Overcoming Common Problems," this book truly empowers couples to take their relationship to the next level of fulfillment and soulful satisfaction.

ISBN 978-08245-2471-5

Please support your local bookstore, or call 1-800-888-4741.
For a free catalog, or to purchase large quantities,
please e-mail us at sales@crossroadpublishing.com

VISIT OUR WEBSITE AT
WWW.CROSSROADPUBLISHING.COM

Other Works by the Author
GREGORY K. POPCAK, PH.D.

GOD HELP ME! THIS STRESS IS DRIVING ME CRAZY!
Finding Balance Through God's Grace

Reduce anxiety and stress by discovering God's healing grace.
In this book you'll find:
- Real-life stories and anecdotes showing how you can deal with stress.
- Checklists, quizzes, and questionnaires to help you identify your own situation.
- Clear explanations of the latest psychological research on stress.
- Insights into how the sacraments enrich your life.
- Reminders of why God is more powerful than even your deepest trouble.

ISBN 978-0-8245-2598-9

Please support your local bookstore, or call 1-800-888-4741.
For a free catalog, or to purchase large quantities,
please e-mail us at sales@crossroadpublishing.com

VISIT OUR WEBSITE AT
WWW.CROSSROADPUBLISHING.COM